HOW TO KNOW...

IS HE OR SHE THE <u>RIGHT</u> ONE?

Nancy H. Brown

WESTBOW
PRESS®
A DIVISION OF THOMAS NELSON
& ZONDERVAN

WestBow Press books may be ordered
through booksellers or by contacting:

WestBow Press
A Division of Thomas Nelson & Zondervan
1663 Liberty Drive
Bloomington, IN 47403
www.westbowpress.com
844-714-3454

ISBN: 978-1-6642-6424-3 (sc)
ISBN: 978-1-6642-6423-6 (e)

Library of Congress Control Number: 2022907373

Print information available on the last page.

WestBow Press rev. date: 5/24/2022

A critical question for sincere Christian singles is: How can I be sure that I marry the right person? Can I know <u>for</u> <u>sure</u> if this is the <u>right</u> man or woman for me?

If you are earnestly asking—in prayer—is this the right man or woman for me; that is a wonderful question for you to ask the Lord!. He wants you to ask, and He wants you to know, if this person is the right one for you. I congratulate you for asking and praying.

The Bible gives some very helpful guidelines in the area of MATE CHOICE and for DECISION-MAKING in general. On the basis of these guidelines, a Christian single can, indeed, be quite sure of making the right choice.

What basic guideline does the Bible offer?

1) Is He Or She Born-again?

The Bible clearly states that a believer is to marry <u>only</u> another believer. In 2 Corinthians 6:14–15, we read:

> Do not be yoked with unbelievers. For what do righteousness and wickedness have in common? Or what fellowship can light have with darkness? What does a believer have in common with an unbeliever? (NIV)

This issue of choosing only a born-again believer needs to be settled for every Christian single who wants to marry in God's will. Jews in the Old Testament were forbidden to intermarry with Canaanites or with people from surrounding nations. Those people worshipped <u>other</u> gods. A marriage alliance to a non-believer was forbidden so that the believer would not be pulled away from affection from the one true God, Jehovah, or from belief in Him. God has never changed His mind in this area. Nor does He make special exceptions.

Human nature has not changed since that time.

People can be and are seduced away from their allegiance and commitment now, just as much as in biblical times.

Solomon in his wisdom said:

> Above all else, guard your affections. For they influence everything else in your life (Proverbs 4:23 TLB)

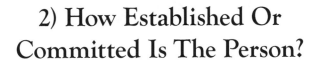

2) How Established Or Committed Is The Person?

Another factor to consider in choosing a mate is the <u>maturity</u> of the other believer. Is he or she a <u>doer</u> of the Word, as well as a hearer? Does he or she actively seek God's will in decision-making, or does this person just verbally assent to wanting to do God's will? Does he or she have a readiness to repent if some area of sin is revealed?

Men or women who are not in the habit of repenting or humbling themselves before God will not be likely to humble themselves in relationships either. But <u>wonderful</u> things can happen in a marriage if both a husband and wife can admit their fault and are willing to say, "I was wrong! Will you forgive me?"

At this point, a reader might be thinking, *Are these characteristics of spiritual maturity true in <u>my</u> life? Am I where I need to be spiritually in order to be a good partner to a wife or husband?*

Those are good questions to ask, and they need to be asked and answered! The time to take inventory is <u>before</u> a person becomes committed or engaged. The unattached single reading this booklet is at a great advantage in the area of choosing because he or she has the option to grow and change and to become a better candidate!! If one's inventory reveals that he or she comes up on the short side in terms of obedience, humility, yieldedness, and so forth, then the appropriate place to start is to ask God for help in shaping the person in those deep areas of the heart that need to be changed to become a compatible and loving partner.

Let's suppose now that the one seeking a mate is a dedicated and mature believer. Is it wise for a mature believer to marry a "baby Christian"? Again, Paul says clearly that <u>equal</u> <u>yoking</u> will produce the best results in a relationship. The brand new Christian has not undergone any testing or persecution. The parable of the sower tells us that many who readily receive the Word fall away when persecution arises for the Word's sake. There is the risk that a new Christian may discard his or her faith when the going gets rough. This is not to say that a marriage between an established believer and a new believer could not work out—especially if the mature believer is the man who is in the position of leadership in the relationship and could guide and nurture his wife as a new believer.

Many such relationships have been successful. It is important, however, to have clear and strong leading from the Lord—especially if the more mature believer is the woman. There is a need for realistic expectations of what adjustments are needed. Much of a new believer's attention and energy will be taken up in growth and change as a Christian, as well as in the adjustments of the marriage itself.

3) Are There Other Areas Of Equal Yoking?

S tatistics indicate that the more a man and woman have in common (background, race, educational interests, religious beliefs, career interests, hobbies, and even physical characteristics [for example, both the man and woman are tall], the longer they are inclined to remain together.

The more interest that the two have to bind them together, the greater the likelihood that they will stay together. There is definite benefit in two people having several areas of sameness. The fewer areas that two people have in common, the <u>less likely</u> it is that they will have a long and enduring relationship. The old expression "opposites attract" may be true, but opposites don't necessarily have lasting relationships. <u>Far</u> opposites may have a much harder time staying together on a long-term basis. The statistics or odds are against a lasting union. There are, of course, exceptions. The statistics referred to speak of the general trend and not of every individual case. There are cases of opposites in marriage who have happy and lasting relationships. The calling of God and the leading of the Holy Spirit, again, are of utmost importance, but it seems wise also to keep in mind that <u>numerous common interests and values</u> are a help in creating a happy and lasting relationship.

The principle of equal yoking is a sound and proven principle both in Scripture and in life in general. To violate this principle is to stack the odds against one's self. It is essential to have equal yoking in the areas of basic beliefs, commitment, and spiritual maturity. Other factors of unequal yoking may hinder the relationship, but they do not have the ability to divide a relationship at its foundation the way the issue of basic beliefs does.

Assuming now that a person is considering only a mate who is genuinely born-again and strongly committed, are there further guidelines to indicate whether a particular person is a good match? Yes, there are guidelines, and God has provided us with clear and helpful ways of knowing the right path to follow.

4) What Does God Want?

This step in decision-making sounds amazingly simple, but it is a step that — for some reason — many Christians totally ignore. This step is simply to ask God His opinion. God wants us to ask Him what He thinks and what He wants. He is complimented when we ask Him! He is honored! He is also grieved and dishonored when we <u>don't</u> ask Him. God has no desire to hide His will from any one of us. He <u>will</u> answer us, and <u>He will reveal</u> His will to us. If there is any problem in our not finding or knowing His will, that problem would be ours and not His.

Our asking Him is also not — or should not be — an option. Proverbs 3:5b – 6 says:

> Lean not unto thine own understanding. In all thy ways acknowledge him, and he shall direct thy paths. (KJV)

The fact is that many Christians <u>do not</u> ask God His opinion or His will in many areas of daily living. Many ask only in the really big areas of life. Some ask only when there is trouble or a crisis. However, Proverbs says:

> <u>In all thy ways</u> acknowledge Him... (Prov.3:6a KJV) (underlining is mine).

I believe it is very important to consider for just a moment <u>why</u> many of us do not ask God His opinion on a daily basis and in most of our decisions.

Many of us assume that we shouldn't bother God with our <u>little</u> decisions, but that assumption can lead to disaster. Why? It's the little decisions that influence and can change the bigger decisions. Little decisions totally alter the future! All of us at some time have had the experience of being in the middle of a mess or a complicated entanglement, and we wonder, *"How did I get here? I never intended to get into <u>this</u>!"* We ended up in those situations because we didn't ask what <u>He</u> wanted us to do. By not asking in the little things — and especially at the <u>beginning</u> of things and relationships — we can end up in huge messes.

I encourage singles to ask God <u>at the beginning</u> of any relationship what <u>He</u> wants before a strong attachment develops — before hand-holding, kissing, or any other physical expressions of affection. Waiting until two days before a wedding is too late for most people to back out in case His answer is NO. That is not the best time to ask, "Lord, is this Your will?" (But even then it is still not too late to back out if the relationship is wrong. Backing out is still a better path than spending a lifetime in unhappiness!) Another reason why many don't ask God for direction is the basic issue of control. Many have never really settled the matter of <u>who</u> is in control. The natural and unregenerate person wants the control of his or her own life.

Many Christians want to be in control and inwardly resent or resist giving that control over to the Holy Spirit. I was this way myself for most of my Christian life. For many years

I did not trust the voice of the Holy Spirit and trusted only my own decisions. Often, when I would hear that inner voice, I would think to myself, *"Hmm, is that a good idea or not?"* I would weigh any suggestions based on my own experience in life, or I would ask myself, *"Do I want to follow that suggestion or not?"* Basically, if I liked the idea and felt favorable to the message or suggestion, I would respond with obedience, and if I didn't like the idea, I ignored it. That was not exactly what Jesus had in mind when He said (referring to Himself as the Shepherd):

> The sheep follow him:
> for they know his voice.
> (John 10:4b KJV)

I perceive that those of us who did not learn to trust (and, therefore, obey willingly—from the heart) our parents early in life have an especially hard time in learning to accept and follow the leading of the Holy Spirit . In my case, it was only after having ended up in one failure after another that I realized and finally accepted the fact that I was doing a miserable job at running my life. It was then that I was truly willing to trust for the first time that still, small, inner voice.

For any believer who has not learned to hear and follow (obey) the leading of the Holy Spirit, I strongly suggest getting this issue settled before seriously pursuing any marriage relationship. If you now find yourself at that place in your Christian experience, you might pray something like the following prayer:

> "Lord, I admit that I don't know how to hear Your voice or distinguish it from my own voice or the voice of "the stranger" (the devil). Sometimes—or often—when I <u>do know</u> it is Your voice, I really don't want to obey or give the control of my life over to You. Would You help me first <u>to want to give You the control</u>? Will You help me to trust You, deep in my spirit, and to want Your will more than my own?

Will You help me to distinguish Your voice from the voice of the enemy?"

If you mean that prayer in all sincerity, God will answer it! Coming to a place of acceptance and trust won't happen in a day, but a process will begin that <u>will bring you to that place</u>!

When I am at a very serious point of wanting to hear from God on a certain issue, I say to the Lord something like the following:

> "Lord, I am willing to do Your will, whatever it is. If You want me to go to the right, I'll go to the right. If You want me to go to the left, I'll go to the left. I will do whatever You want me to do, but please show me clearly what Your will is."

When I approach God with this kind of seriousness for obedience, He <u>always</u> speaks to me. In following this pattern, He has saved and spared me from one trap or snare after another, and has consistently led and drawn me in the direction that He has wanted me to go. Hallelujah!! Had I been only half in earnest, or playing games, or deceiving myself, then God might not have spoken at all. God is not compelled to answer us if we are asking out of <u>mere curiosity</u>. Jeremiah wrote:

> And ye shall seek me, and find me, when ye shall search for me with all your heart
> (Jeremiah 29:13 KJV).

It is basically a mockery of God and an insult to Him to ask His will and to ignore it or reject it. What consequences will result if the believer does not come to this place of trust and obedience?

> 1) He or she will be left to rely on his or her own experience, wisdom, and knowledge—which for all of us is ever so limited—for the outcome of any relationship.

2) He or she will not have the advantage of divine insight and foreknowledge that would be of the utmost importance in making a decision with such far-reaching consequences.

3) He or she will be subject to the element of <u>deception</u> which is the enemy's basic tactic for ensnaring and destroying the Christian!

5) Do I Have Peace?

The Bible says <u>peace</u> is an element that we should aim for in <u>all</u> situations, and it plays a key role in all decision-making. God has created us so that our inner spirits give us signals. If we listen to those inner messages, they may give a STOP, a GO, or a WAIT signal as clearly as a traffic light would in the natural realm. A message of a peaceful, contented, inward quietness is a very good indication that a relationship has a good foundation and may have a good future. This Peace is different from the excitement or thrill of the other person's touch or caress. It is totally different from sexual excitement. This peace is a deep inner sense of comfort in being with the other person over a prolonged period of time. (Two dates is too short a time to make this judgment!). The presence of this peace is vital in our <u>leading</u>. Anything that seems like a <u>troubled spirit</u> or a recurring area of worry, anxiety, or agitation is meant as a warning sign to wait, be cautious, or to investigate further before proceeding. Our inner spirits can warn us of trouble or danger ahead <u>if we will listen</u> to our own signals.

If peace is lacking, there is always a serious reason why! As humans, we are blessed with our own inner <u>antenna</u>. Consider the following Scriptures in regard to peace:

> Seek peace, and pursue it
> (Ps. 34:14b NASB)

> ....God has called us to peace
> (1 Cor. 7:15b NASB)

> Try to live in peace even if you must run after it to catch and hold it! (I Peter 3:11 TLB)

> ...follow after the things which make for peace
> (Romans 14:19 KJV)

The presence of peace—or lack of it—can serve as a test in the decision-making process. If peace <u>rules</u> the spirit regarding a certain person, then we have another <u>go ahead</u> from Scripture. But, if recurring areas of worry or anxiety prevail, the person considering marriage needs to stop! To go ahead and ignore a <u>check</u> in one's spirit or a gnawing, troublesome feeling is to ask for disaster.

God is gracious to warn us of a coming mistake, but we must heed His warnings. Many believers have not listened to their own spirits' signals and have ended up in misery and divorce court. This principle is also tested and true:

> For the kingdom of God is...
> righteousness, and <u>peace</u>, and
> joy in the Holy Ghost
> (Underlining is mine)
> (Romans 14:17 KJV)

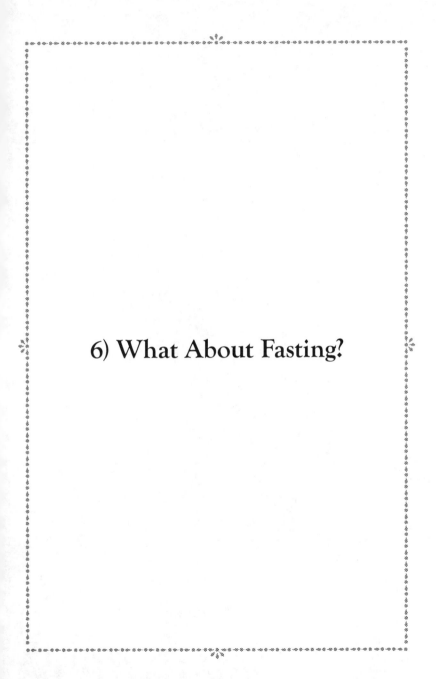

6) What About Fasting?

One of the greatest benefits of fasting is that it can help to cut through confusion and deception that may surround a situation. For that reason, it can be a highly valuable tool for a Christian single who needs more <u>light</u> in a situation. It actually seems foolish for someone who is contemplating marriage <u>not</u> to take advantage of this mighty spiritual weapon. Again, however, the person must really <u>want</u> God's will. If a person's mind is already made up, and he or she doesn't really want to know God's will, then there is no point in fasting.

I recommend fasting even when all circumstance seem to be ideal! Why?? The <u>appearance</u> of circumstances can be very misleading. Someone who appears to be an ideal future partner could be a secret drinker, a man or woman-hater, or a con artist who is doing his or her best to put up a good front. Fasting can open the way for hidden or secret things to surface.

Take, for example, the case of Shelly (not her real name) who had been praying for a husband and developed a crush on Doug (not his real name) at a local Christian ministry where they both worked. Shelly reached a kind of deadlock in her relationship with Doug, and after much prayer felt frustrated in not being able to go forward in getting to know him. At that point, she decided to fast and ask God for special revelation regarding the relationship. As she did, she was willing to let the relationship go forward, or to let it drop if it were not the right one for her. After a period of fasting, she described her answer as something like this:

> "Because of the fasting, I was listening for any word from the Lord. I remember walking into the bathroom on a Friday night after work. As I stepped up to the sink, I heard that special voice as clear as anything saying that the door is closed <u>because he has closed it</u>, and I need to

be grateful that he closed it! If he ever wants to open it for me, he will open it! At first I was in shock, not really having wanted a negative answer, but at the same time I was thrilled with the unmistakable assurance that Almighty God <u>Himself</u> had spoken to me!! There was no doubt in my mind that the message could have been from Him alone. I could actually feel His love, concern, and protection in that response.

Within a few more weeks, Doug left the company, and no reasons were ever given as to why he left the company.

How grateful I am for God's protection. I know for certain that just as clearly as He spoke to me in this situation, He will let me know when the right man comes along."

What a great testimony of God's faithfulness and His leading!

Does He speak as clearly, though, when it is the right person and the right match? One well-known radio speaker, who has had a Gospel ministry for years and a special outreach in Israel, recounts that exact situation. He had met a lovely Christian woman and felt–after a month of fasting–that God had showed him clearly that he was to marry her. They continue in fruitful and successful ministry today.

Once again the basic issue is that God is willing to and does lead, but are we willing to listen and to follow? Are we willing to let go of our plans if God reveals that such plans would hurt us or make us unhappy? Are we willing to trust Him and the wisdom and goodness in His nature even when we can't see the reasons why? Are we willing to let Him control and guide? If the answer to those questions is NO, then we could be setting ourselves up for major hurt. If the answer is NO, then we ourselves may not be ready for commitment and responsibility of marriage. It is a major step in our spiritual life to want <u>His will</u> more than we want our own will. It is a major breakthrough in faith and obedience when we reach the point of <u>trusting</u> His leading–even if it conflicts with our fleshly desires and sometimes those long and–as yet–unfulfilled, <u>good</u> desires.

But let's get back to the issue of fasting. If one has never fasted before, this experience does not have to be dreadful or overly rigorous physical denial. However, it is always–to some degree–a denial of self and the flesh. A fast can be as short as one or two meals, or it may involve giving up some other pleasures for a period of time. It can involve anything that will serve as a reminder of prayer. Food abstinence can involve a variety of choices varying from eating only light meals with no desserts, to eating no meals and only water or fruit juices, to a forty-day fast. Even in cases where a rigorous work schedule is involved, it is still possible to eat limited sustenance items, but give up all luxury items.

My first fast began by giving up all sweets and desserts for a period of two weeks. For me at that time, that was a big step! It amazed me at that time–and still does–how greatly God honored that fast! My purpose was to receive direction as to whether or not I should renew for one year a contract in the job I was in at the time. On the second to the last day of the fast, I experienced an amazing breakthrough! On that day, a major scandal was revealed in the life of the boss in connection with the company. As a result, it was clear to me what decision I should make. I chose <u>not</u> to renew my contract for the following year, but moved on to seek a new job. From that experience, I saw first-hand how valuable and helpful fasting could be—especially at decision time. I have been an enthusiastic promoter of fasting even since.

For the person who has never fasted at all, I suggest starting with a short period of time and fasting just a few meals. It is important to ask God: "What do <u>You</u> want me to give up? For how long of a period do I need to fast and pray?" For the Christian who is willing to seek an answer through this means, there will be a breakthrough of light and <u>direction!</u> God honors fasting!

What Next?

For the reader who may be at a fork in the road today, I encourage serious consideration of these questions:

1) Is the one I am considering a genuine born-again believer?

2) Is that one a <u>doer</u> of the Word? Does he or she have a will that is yielded to the Lord?

3) Do the two of us have some—or a number—of interests in common or similar background characteristics?

4) Do I (and he or she) have a sense of sustained peace and rightness about this relationship over an extended period of time?

5) Have I (and he or she) asked God step by step what <u>He</u> wants, and have we received an affirmative answer?

6) Am I (and he or she) willing to fast and seek a definite go-ahead from God before committing to this person in regard to marriage?

If the answer to all of these questions is YES, then there should and will be a great sense of freedom and confidence in going forward into marriage. There is no substitute in life for the joy in knowing that we are <u>in His perfect will!</u> What security that gives for facing the future! The place of wholeheartedness is a happy place to be!

As believers, we need to be whole-hearted in making a lifetime commitment. May God bless every reader with wholeheartedness, joy, and deep inner assurance in making this all-important decision!

****

Making Sure Of Salvation

Perhaps as a reader today someone may be wondering, *"Am I a Christian? I think I may be, but I'm not sure."* Or, perhaps another reader may know for sure that he or she is not a Christian or that he or she has never made a commitment to Jesus Christ. If you are one of those individuals and want to become a Christian (or if you want the wonderful benefit of being able to be led by the Holy Spirit in <u>all</u> of your relationships), you can settle that decision once and for all. Salvation comes by inviting Jesus Christ to live in your heart by faith and by confessing with your mouth that He is Lord. If you wish to take that step and settle forever the matter of your salvation, would you pray this prayer now?

> Dear Lord, I confess that I am a sinner, and I need your forgiveness. I've done a lot of things wrong, and I've said a lot of bad things. I ask you to totally wash me and cleanse me. I believe that Jesus Christ is the son of God and that He

died on the cross <u>in my place</u> to pay the penalty for my sin. I receive Him now as my Savior and Lord and I invite the Holy Spirit to come into my heart and live in me forever. Thank you, Lord, for saving me. Will you show me how to walk with You day by day?

(Date of My Spiritual Birthday)

Verses to help with assurance of salvation:

… God has given us eternal life and this life is in his Son. So whoever has God's Son has life; whoever does not have his Son, does not have life. I have written this to you who believe in the Son of God so that you may know you have eternal life." (I John 5:11–13 TLB)

Begin Sharing Today

If you have been helped in the area of mate choice or some other area, please share this booklet right away with another person! In blessing someone else, you will yourself receive a great blessing. Proverbs tells us,

> He that waterth shall be watered
> also himself
> (Proverbs 11:25 KJV)

About the Author

Nancy H. Brown, B.A., M.A., public school educator for English and history; College instructor for writing; hospital chaplain; singles group leader and counsellor; short term missionary to Ethiopia, Dominican Republic, Russia, and more; poet and public speaker.

At age 14 Nancy was invited by a middle school teacher to attend a Billy Graham Gospel meeting at the Detroit Fair Grounds. At that meeting she committed her life to

Christ, which began a series of positive changes, helping her to survive a difficult home life and to begin her own personal healing and growth.

After moving to Denver, she started chaplain work with on the job training. Denver also became home to a singles group and more positive people contacts.

Years later in Southern California, Nancy continued teaching and chaplain work. At a large Los Angeles hospital, Nancy worked for years in the Cancer Clinic, with patients with all levels of cancer. She also taught classes on "Ministering to the Sick and Winning the Lost".

Nancy has always enjoyed working with people of all ages, races, and nationalities.

Printed in the United States
by Baker & Taylor Publisher Services